The Grief Collective

Words for the grief collective undergoing an impoverished existence underneath the oligarchy

Emily Larson

BookLeaf Publishing

India | USA | UK

Copyright © Emily Larson
All Rights Reserved.

This book has been self-published with all reasonable efforts taken to make the material error-free by the author. No part of this book shall be used, reproduced in any manner whatsoever without written permission from the author, except in the case of brief quotations embodied in critical articles and reviews.

The Author of this book is solely responsible and liable for its content including but not limited to the views, representations, descriptions, statements, information, opinions, and references ["Content"]. The Content of this book shall not constitute or be construed or deemed to reflect the opinion or expression of the Publisher or Editor. Neither the Publisher nor Editor endorse or approve the Content of this book or guarantee the reliability, accuracy, or completeness of the Content published herein and do not make any representations or warranties of any kind, express or implied, including but not limited to the implied warranties of merchantability, fitness for a particular purpose.

The Publisher and Editor shall not be liable whatsoever...

Made with ❤ on the BookLeaf Publishing Platform
www.bookleafpub.in
www.bookleafpub.com

Dedication

This chapbook is for all Americans living, suffering, and maintaining through poverty. May our stories be heard and shared with the world.

Preface

Go back to nature; she's waiting for you.

Acknowledgements

My greatest wishes for a calm and peaceful life go out to all who have supported and encouraged me on my journey thus far. I deeply admire my chosen sister, Marissa Wilson, for helping me heal through rupture and repair and teaching me to believe in my innermost being. I want to thank Val Laster and Tricia Kregg for taking a chance on me and always being there to root for me. My gratitude goes out to all my English and Literature professors and teachers. Thank you for encouraging my writing and teaching about the written word's impact on lives and societies.

1. Societies Shame

Shame in feeling the ache
Shame in hiding alone,
Shame on being hungry,
Shame on asking for more.

Faced with the realization that I'm afraid to approach others
In an ill state;
To be sedated or worse-
Shunned for sharing such a heavy burden onto their shoulders
Fearful that my voice won't construct the same sounds that play in my mind
That my words won't make sense to them.

Shame on the fear
Shame on the trust
Shame on loving too much
Shame on the success
Shame for the stuck
Shame on the still
Shame in the rush

Today, I awoke feeling a great sense of heaviness,

within this, I sunk into the feeling of body;
The aches and pains that accompany it
The feeling of heavy stillness.
I saw myself days and weeks before,
Consumed by the mind
Aching in another way
Pain in familiar form

Shame on being homesick
Shame on wandering alone
Shame on loving deeply
Shame on vulnerability
Shame on letting go
Shame on remembering

Shame on the past
Shame for the dread of living
Shame on the future
The then
The next
The last

Shame on indecision
Shame on the choice
Shame on the shaking of my voice

Why is it always

Seemingly
Achingly
Night
When I reach out to hear you speak?
I won't dismiss or disturb
The restless heart is a place for worship,
Instead, I see a home with a locked door.

Shame on running from the past
Shame on running to whom I've become
Shame on pretending to be anything different
Shame to be anything at all.

Today, I awoke, my heart fluttering fast,
all-consuming anxiety before my brain could speak;
What haven't I achieved?
I lead myself back to sleep.
No need to be awake,
No need to run,
No need to weep.

Shame on the debt
Shame on the trust
Shame on the hope
Shame on the lust.

Shame to wait-

It's just me.
No gods, no goddesses to be seen
In this
Ominous,
Deafening void we call
Reality.

I lie to say I am at peace with whatever may be;

Shame to be me.

2. Clash of the Brains

You scoffed when I told you,
Our brains aren't symmetrical.
Diametrically opposed,
Socioeconomic standoff at the dining table.

Your words dance,
Prancing off your tongue as though they were rehearsed.
I reach to grab a line, and it slips from my memory,
I hold tight the ones I catch with a shakey grasp.

I repeat it, I repeat it.

Your eyes dart, my heart races, I search for something-
Anything,
What is off?
Amygdala scrambling the nervous system,
Cortisol pumping through my blood.
I reach for your hand,
You retract.
My sight seems to be worsening,
Glitching as I flinch back.

I apologize,
I apologize

But I can't remember what for.

Mouth open to speak,
I stutter,
You glare
My words seem out of order,
The thoughts fade into your gaze
You retort,
If I start crying, I will not be able to stop,
So I smile,
As if there is anything else I can do,

My hippocampus surely doesn't work for me,
Why should it perform for you?

3. Not a Love Letter

It's not a love letter. It can't be,
There's a coffee stain on it.
It's not a love letter,
You've heard these words uttered thousands of moons
before,
And can still feel it in your aching bones.
I see the streets around me unrecognizable
But so familiar
There's something more intense about it now.
Now, the protests are silenced by the
Inability to scream
While continuously adapting,
Constantly surviving,
Finding,
Loosing,
Needing,
Loathing.
Aching.

I walk around unfamiliar, cold, plastic suburbs,
And ask the earth and the trees and
Anything
Anything
To help me

The wind rustles, and I am content with this response,
I cling to this feeling;
Peace,
Acceptance,
Surrender.

Many people are lounging in chairs,
Watching missiles explode on the news.
I think about how the people from the city may come up
here,
During the impending class warfare
But the suburbs have guns,
And the city sedates us.
It turns us bitter and unwilling to want better for
ourselves,
Because it has been shown time and time again that we
cannot help ourselves,
It is futile.

They position us with the food we are given
With the water we drink
Poverty produces enough cortisol to stop a horse's heart,
With how we slave away for corporations.
But you've already heard that.
Of course, you've already heard that.
You know that.
That's why I'm writing you.

I like to think about the things I want in life,
It gives me some control over things.

But what I truly need is this here;
A surrender to sirens and screams,
An arm steady enough to fall upon when I feel I've lost
my own,
To know eternally that I am not alone.
So I want to tell you
You are not alone,
You are forever supported and loved deeply,
You are not abnormal,
You are not a robot.
Life will support you through whatever may happen.
You will find love everywhere,
We are all here,
Collectively,
Feeling the urge to move,
Without the strength to do so.

It is not your fault.
We cannot do this alone,
We need each other.
And I need you to know how strong we are together,
As two people,
As a society,
As a collective,

Mind and Energy.
We are only alone as they will us to be.
But we are stronger.
As long as our hands can clasp onto one another,
As long as we keep breathing,
I know we are stronger.
So we will it to change,
And it will change.
So we will the courage to love,
And love surrounds us.

Yours truly,

Restless, Willing, Poisoned

4. Meeting of The Winds

One harsh winter's day, I was born into a blizzard,
I met the Winds clashing about,
I was brought inside,
Safety.
I grew up with the Wind rushing against
Chapped lips
Bitter on my skin,
Like a knife to a peach
I learned to be made of wood,
Able to be carved out at any expense,
I would listen to it scream outside my window,
I would feel it seep in through the walls.
The Wind was not my friend.
I walked home, trudging through the Michigan snow,
Wind swiping against my being as if it could take my
soul.

One day, I left on an airplane
The winds were angry, and the turbulence put me to
sleep
As I knew well the winds to be angry,
Unkind,
Unable to greet.

When I awoke in Switzerland, the Wind had died down,
and all around me was
Silence,
Retreat.
I awoke each day, awaiting the Wind to return
It did not,
Each day, I felt an ominous yearning for when we would
again meet.

Until one day, I hiked up the mountains,
Up and up, even though I felt I could not breathe,
Up to where the ice claves of the alp side and I did meet.
And I stood as I felt a great presence about,
The Wind started to pick up.
It began with a whistle,
I braced myself for what was to come.
It hummed about through the mountains,
I introduced myself to it,
And it sang for me.
No whipping or slashing,
Just a song,
Just a recognition that I was seen.

The Wind and I spoke for many minutes,
Then all fell silent,
I journeyed on through the snow,
Carried now by the Wind's gentle and powerful calm.

5. The Waiting Room

Lie awake,
Stare at the walls,
Create stories in your mind,
They'll tell you you're creative,
Bright.
You wait.
In the bed,
To be allowed out of the room.
In the bed,
For them to wake up.
In the bed,
sheets unwashed,
tearing your hair out.
You wait.

In the hospital room,
Isolated and bright,
Nothing interesting to look at,
Too much noise,
Sterile and stern.
You wait.

In the office,
For your name to be called,

For your audition,
Pick me, you say,
As you dance for them,
Answering the questions
With correct punctuation

You wait,
In the cubicle you worked so hard
To get into.
You wait,
To be called on in the meeting,
For your report.
You wait,
For love,
For joy,
For inspiration,
For freedom.

You wait
For yourself
You wait.

6. Medicine Man - Psychiatry In America

The Medicine Man tells me I'm sick.
For a paycheck, for the strings that attach him to his
debt.
I feel it is my fault,
He says it is incurable,
Yet gives me pills.
The pills make me ache,
They make me dull and dreary,
Dellusional and Hallucinatory,
The Medicine man tells me I need more pills
To fix these ailments.

And I believe him because I am sick,
And I believe him because he is a doctor.
I take more pills to make me better,
The aching turns to tremors, restless through my
muscles,
The dread turns to wishes of death, darker than the new
moon's rays
The hallucinations turn to full apparitions in the rooms
next to me,
Mermors and names when no one is around.

"

The Medicine Man tells me I need to be shocked to get
better,
That my case is so severe,
That the medication was supposed to help,
That my body was wrong,
That my brain is wrong,
That I am wrong.

The Medicine Man takes me away,
And I am gone.
Gone from the Earth,
Who cries for me to come home,
Gone from the ones who know the same aches,
They await the same fate.
So I tell you now,
Go to the Earth,
The Water,
The Caverns,
Go to the Trees,
Go to the others,
Let them know they are not sick when they can be free,
Tell them to go to where the Medicine Man cannot see.

7. She

We have read about her,
The one who spoke up,
The one who wrote for a cause,
The one who opened her arms to those in need.
We read about her in class,
Her name
Scattered amongst others in the history books.

We say, look how great she did.
Now, nothing has been the same since her dedication to-
We wait,
Nothing has changed, He says.
Back and forth, we say her name,
We rock and sway,
The narrative stays still, He says
The ending to the story never came,
We repeat history, She says
Time and time again,
We say her name.

Until another Her comes about,
We discern and dismiss,
We say without thought,
Without knowledge or reason to dismiss,

"Your name is not familiar,
'Miss.'"

8. The Polar Vortex

I looked for you,
In the blizzard for two weeks straight.
I had socks and a backpack to give you,
Things you said for in which you'd wait.
The last day,
Dropped off at the shelter,
Broken wheelchair,
A handful of pills and a letter.
We sat together,
Trying to jump through the hoops of the system,
You cried, and I thought
Maybe
Next week, you might feel better.
Next week might be the one.

You were rough and bitter,
Rightfully so.
The previous week, you had been stabbed under a bridge,
The next thrown into a random home.
I tried to be your voice,
But it fell short amongst the rage
Of the worker underneath the paperwork,
Of the system set up to immediately DISENGAGE
Ran back to the office to find some gloves,

By the time I found you outside again
You were drunk
To numb from the cold all around.
I told you to take shelter for the night,
That a storm was incoming.
You thanked me and told me you would,
You smiled,
And said to be safe during the storm, too.

I went on my way, did my paperwork that night.
That night you were shoved into a cellar basement,
Concrete floors,
Packed in like sardines,
With the other men who swore,
They told me you had a heart attack there,
Died on the floor.
I looked for you for weeks,
You died on the floor.
I made sure that someone claimed your body
before I wrote your letter for disengagement.
I made sure you were not sent to the landfill of bodies,
I wanted to do more.

9. Schizoaffective Disorder - NGRI

Not Guilty by Reason of Insanity

Is what they started off with
A crime so heinous
They had to be locked away
In State Institutions for the Insane
Instead of chains,
They were given prescriptions,
Sedation.
A decade later, they were released,
Into hallways,
Locked doors,
Three times a day I would call for them,
Medication so strong they would fall into walls,
Collapse into one another,
Yet there was a "hope of re-integration into society."
In their charts, they were labeled as Schizoaffective,
A three-page history of childhood trauma.
Their brains now shrunk and stalled,
Mashed by the drugs.
Integrated into another hallway,
locked doors and stalled time.
Guilty of any attempted escape,

No true return,
Prisoners now of the mind.

10. The Hawk and The Deer

Men in power want to leave the word

Women

Out

Because if we keep it in, we might be reminded that

before God was He

The Earth and Universe was reverend before She

So I go to Her,

And ask,

Does the hawk laugh at the deer while fleeing, following

along in the air?

Does the deer look up at the hawk,

While the hawk wonders why the deer is suddenly so

still?

Does the deer take awe in the hawk's flight?

Does the hawk circle the deer's open and bloody carcass,

After it wandered too deep into the road

Because it feels the pain?

Or is it just for pleasure?

Does the hawk know the deer pays close attention,

And aims to do the same?

Or does it fly without concern of any such thing,

Diving and bobbing through the wind as it soars.

In these woods, no animal besides the deer is quite this

tame.

11. Catching the Breath

I once asked a man in Greece how he survived the
sweltering Greece summers
He said, "breathe."
When I breathe, it doesn't always completely fill up my
chest
There is an ache and a scratch and a suture that hasn't
healed from its
Reoccurring infections

When I see an airplane, I think of myself,
Far away,
I watch it as it fades over the horizon
They say new beginnings are ways to shed your old skin
But what if your skin has been sewn into your organs
So you may grow around it but never from it
How do you accept it
Always aching and itching like that?

My parents told me when I was born, I cried nonstop for
weeks on end
How do I say it never stopped
How do I say I still hear it
And feel it rattle my very being with every breath I try
To take fully

How do I connect with others
When I don't even know my own language

There are glimpses of good memories I have
Now and then
Spring time I buckle up black shoes,
My white socks have lace frills on them
I feel joy as I open the door to the spring air
I think of what happens next
But it's not there
What happened?

Your silence is so loud
Louder than my cries,
Inside,
As the torn skin is sewed onto the lungs
And I am told I must shed it to start anew.

12. Spider Medicine

The spider does not run after anyone
She spins and weaves and creates
There is an inner stillness in her wait
The creation is both alluring, beautiful, and
Hidden
She does not weave for any crowds
Or any beings of the sort to judge the patterns made
She weaves and waits
She weaves and waits
The wind does not startle her
And when the rain and hail comes
She awaits its passing
And quickly rebuilds
She weaves
She waits
I am like the spider
In the sense that when someone falls into my web
I will wrap myself around them
To the point of suffocation
The spider does not release
The spider does not let go
Qualities of hers that others may find unsettling
Yet, in wonderment to me, she doesn't fawn over what is
in her nest

She waits
She weaves
She rests

13. Thoughts on Poverty in Switzerland

How to explain American society to someone who has
only seen us through Hollywood and advertisements:

How do I explain while I'm still choking,
As it appears I'm drowning in the open air?
As I reach for my paperwork for the psychiatrist to
prove
I need these medications for sleep for my insomnia
That I am not just faking it
And he looks a bit perturbed
A bit perplexed
As to why I would need to prove anything
His job was to help
And we talked for two hours
And he told me he had only ever witnessed this much
trauma before
In patients from war zones
As I try to explain America to the psychiatrist
As I try to explain America to the Italian
As I try to explain America to the therapist
As I try to explain America to the Swiss
As I try to explain America to my roommates from
Upper-Class America

As I try to explain America to myself
As we take classes depicting my life
And we inspect how and why
And I listen to others creating interpretations of my life.

14. Comfort

I recall comfort as the snow's mellowed embrace,
Circling around the edges of the world as I saw it.
How the breeze of the night was hushed and smooth,
Like a raindrop rolling off of a leaf somewhere in the deep forest.
The violets and butterflies, moths, and warm sunlight were my comfort
Among the branches and rolling green hills of the neighbor's yard. I pranced and played, laughed and skipped,
I used the plants and sticks as potions and wands. My father yells at me to stop.
They say that fathers are innately playful.
That they feel the call just as mothers feel the need to nurture.
I recall warm Sunday afternoons giggling and running through the house as my father chased me.
When he caught up to me, he would lift me high and laugh with a growl.
The game would go on and on until it was time for supper.
This was before time took them.
This was before poverty took them.
My mother and father took turns running away,

Slamming the door and squealing off in the green car out
of the pebbled driveway and far off out of view.
I think this innately came to them: the need to run.
I recall comfort as a pen to a piece of paper as my mind
wandered and drifted,
As I created in silence as not to be judged or ridiculed,
Cursed or damned into a sin I couldn't escape from.
My punishment was swift and often,
Overwhelming lonely and long.
I would turn to the pages and the pencils I had to escape.
I had learned it was easy to do, even without a green car.

15. A Call to Arms

You may not understand the weight to survive,

But I assure you the riots will come, and there will be a
day of reckoning.

The day will come when you hear our tears, screams, and
wails

As they will echo within the empty cavities between
your ribs.

Teardrops on an empty carcass.

Wails of joy will surround you, bloody and lifeless, just
as you had left us.

16. Reverse Culture Shock - Coming back to the United States from Switzerland

It seems difficult, if not near impossible, to accept that you can live without a water filter or a million supplements to get by, that the feeling of being trapped here, the dread of the reality, is that we are not chosen or destined to live anywhere besides the country we were born in, like cattle born to breed, that we are trapped inside of a money making machine until the day we are slaughtered by the illnesses it has created.

That we may only visit the pastures for brief moments and close our eyes in our kennels once again to dream of the fields we were meant to roam.

17. A Question for The Dead

Was the room closing in on you?
Was there another body there to comfort you?
Were you too weak to ask again for anything?
Did anyone familiar come to get you?

Once you stopped running, did death's embrace swallow
or caress you?
Were you afraid, or did the silence of it all comfort you?
Was it like stepping out into spring air after being
trapped inside for an eternity of winter?

Did you fade,
Or collapse?
Was the fall as long as you'd anticipated?
And your last breath -
Was it met with another,
Or was that it?

Death and I have had many encounters with one
another.
When I try to run, it seems to upset him.
When I am still, he is all-encompassing,
When I look him in the eyes,
I see he means no ill will.

18. The Unhoused

I saw a man lying in a sleeping bag as snow crested on
the damp cardboard box he was lying in.
I saw a woman selling herself for a place to sleep while
dying and constantly crying from grief.
I saw men crowded together in a homeless shelter, like
dogs in a kennel, like sheep in a pen.
I saw people drugged and held in a hallway.
I saw a young man take his own life after the hospital
had discharged him.
His insurance wouldn't cover any more time.
I saw a woman in a trailer, staying with her five children,
sister, and three grandchildren.
I saw men and women being discarded and discharged
while pleading for help.
I saw them screaming and being sedated.
I saw them overdosing.
I saw them crying,
I held their hand,
I lied,
When I said I could help.
I thought I could do something,
Something more than saving money for the insurance
companies,

Something more than saving money for the non-profit
companies,
Something more,
Is what they were to me,
Than money.

19. We must create change. We must create reform.

Let it begin with your story.

Begin with a hum,
Then, a whisper,
Then a word.
Make it disarranged,
Dellusional and aggressive,
Assertive and demanding.

Make a sound.
If nothing else,
Make a sound.

May this be your guiding light,
May you have the loudest voice in this dreary, long
night.
May your heart be whole with gratitude for what has not
yet come.
May you know your true birthright to speak.
May you be heard.
May you be heard.
May you be heard.

Speak.

www.ingramcontent.com/pod-product-compliance
Lightning Source LLC
Chambersburg PA
CBHW061727130726
47996CB00006B/2530